Lerner SPORTS

BEHIND THE SCENES
SOCCER

by Andy Greder

Lerner Publications ◆ Minneapolis

Lerner Publications Company
A division of Lerner Publishing Group, Inc.
241 First Avenue North
Minneapolis, MN 55401 USA

For reading levels and more information, look up this title at www.lernerbooks.com.

The images used in this book are used with the permission of: © Rich Graessle/Icon Sportswire/Corbis/Getty Images, p. 1; © Ira L. Black/Corbis/Corbis Sport/Getty Images, pp. 4–5, 6; © Rob Marmion/Shutterstock.com, pp. 8–9; © Shawn Patrick Ouellette/Portland Press Herald/Getty Images, pp. 10–11; © Robin Alam/Icon Sportswire/Getty Images, p. 13; © Meg Oliphant/Getty Images Sport/Getty Images, pp. 14–15; © Dave Winter/Icon Sport/Getty Images, p. 17; © Kyodo News/Getty Images, p. 19; © Serena Taylor/Newcastle United/Getty Images, pp. 20–21; © Franck Fife/AFP/Getty Images, p. 22; © Tim Clayton/Corbis/Corbis Sport/Getty Images, pp. 24–25; © Marco Rosi/Getty Images Sport/Getty Images, p. 27; © MShev/Shutterstock.com, p. 29.

Front cover: © Rich Graessle/Icon Sportswire/Corbis/Getty Images.

Main body text set in Myriad Pro.
Typeface provided by Adobe.

Library of Congress Cataloging-in-Publication Data

Names: Greder, Andy, 1983– author.
Title: Behind the scenes soccer / Andy Greder.
Description: Minneapolis : Lerner Publications, [2020] | Series: Inside the sport |
Includes bibliographical references and index. | Audience: Ages: 7–11. | Audience: Grades: 4–6.
Identifiers: LCCN 2018052619 (print) | LCCN 2019000006 (ebook) | ISBN 9781541556317 (eb pdf) | ISBN 9781541556072 (lb : alk. paper) |
    ISBN 9781541574397 (pb : alk. paper)
Subjects: LCSH: Soccer—Juvenile literature. | Soccer—Training—Juvenile literature. | Soccer players—Juvenile literature.
Classification: LCC GV943.25 (ebook) | LCC GV943.25 .G73 2020 (print) | DDC 796.334—dc23

LC record available at https://lccn.loc.gov/2018052619

Manufactured in the United States of America
1-CG-7/15/19

CONTENTS

WINNING THE CHAMPIONSHIP

On a cold, windy day in December 2017, Toronto FC hosted the Seattle Sounders in the Major League Soccer (MLS) final. It was a rematch. A year earlier, Seattle had crushed the hopes of the home fans by winning the title in a penalty kick shootout. Star midfielder Michael Bradley and his Toronto FC teammates were determined not to let it happen two years in a row.

Toronto pushed hard in the first half, but Seattle's goalkeeper was up to the task. Finally, midway through the second half, Toronto broke through with a goal.

Michael Bradley helps Toronto FC win the MLS Cup in 2017. ▶

FACTS
at a Glance

- Young soccer players can take many different paths to become professionals.

- Pro soccer players often eat foods rich in carbohydrates for energy.

- Soccer players can run up to eight miles in a game.

- Most pro soccer players do strength training off the field to stay strong.

- Soccer is known for its loyal fans.

Bradley and the rest of the Toronto FC players cheer after winning the MLS Cup trophy.

The crowd went wild. Another late goal clinched the game and gave Toronto FC the championship.

Bradley grabbed the silver MLS Cup trophy with both hands and raised it over his head. A blizzard of confetti poured down onto him as the fans roared. Bradley brought the shiny cup back down and kissed it.

Bradley started playing soccer with his father at an early age. His dad was a professional soccer coach. Bradley tagged along to practices to clean shoes and fetch balls for the players. He did anything he could to be a part of the game. When he got older, he often joined practice.

Bradley went on to become captain of the US Men's National Team and a midfielder for Toronto FC. But he didn't become a star overnight. The best soccer players put in hours of practice. They prepare off the field too, with healthful meals and hard workouts. They try to win Olympic or World Cup medals. Some win the MLS Cup like Bradley.

CHAPTER 1

BECOMING A PRO

Many professional soccer players started playing at about five years old. But some started even earlier. Christian Pulisic, who plays for the US Men's National Team, began kicking a soccer ball before he was two years old. Carli Lloyd, who has won two Olympic gold medals with the US Women's National Team, started playing when she was five.

There are many ways to become a professional soccer player. Some play in high school and college before playing professionally. The best young players may be picked to join the Olympic Development Program. That is a huge honor for a soccer player.

Soccer is a popular sport for people of all ages. ▶

Teenagers who want to play soccer professionally ▶ practice a lot.

Playing on the Olympic development team gives players experience against the toughest competition. It also allows scouts from college and professional teams to watch them play.

By the time they're teenagers, most serious players give up other sports and play only soccer. Some young soccer players join elite travel teams. Some of those elite players are scouted to join professional teams' youth academies. When Pulisic was sixteen, he joined the academy for Borussia Dortmund in Germany's top soccer league. He still played for that team in 2018, along with playing for the US Men's National Team. Most players never go pro. But those who do can play in the United States or in other countries.

Some American men's soccer players start their professional careers in the United Soccer League (USL). The pay is low, so they coach soccer or have other part-time jobs to make extra money. The best soccer players move up to MLS. Americans and players from other countries in MLS earn at least $55,000 each year. But some players earn millions.

For women's soccer players, the best opportunity to play in the United States is in the National Women's Soccer League (NWSL). They can also play for the US Women's National Team. That team is among the best in the world. Some women also play in overseas professional leagues.

Carli Lloyd works
hard as a midfielder
for the US Women's
National Team.

CHAPTER 2

A TYPICAL GAME DAY

Soccer players have a lot to think about on game day. To start, they watch what they eat before the game. Christen Press, a forward on the US Women's National Team, likes to eat an omelet with meats, vegetables, and cheese. Lloyd likes to eat a salad before games. Many other players choose to eat pasta. Pasta is rich in carbohydrates that the body can digest quickly. Most soccer players eat their pregame meal about four hours before the game. They drink water with their meal to stay hydrated.

Players on the US Women's National Team stretch before a big game. ▶

Stats Spotlight
2 to 8

That's about how many miles soccer players run during a game. Midfielders cover the most distance, at about 7 or 8 miles (11.3 or 12.9 km) per game. Wide defenders run 5 to 6 miles (8 to 9.7 km). Forwards and center defenders run about 5 miles (8 km). In one 2018 game, the goalkeeper ran about 2 miles.

Players arrive at the stadium about two hours early to prepare for the game. The locker room is a quiet place where players begin to focus. They might listen to music with headphones. Press likes to meditate for twenty minutes. This keeps her calm before the game. Coaches also use this time to talk to players. They often discuss game plans they outlined during training earlier that week.

Players take the field for about twenty-five minutes before the game. They warm up by stretching and running through drills. Fans start to fill the stadium. Music is often playing overhead.

Then the players return to the locker room to change into their uniforms. They drink water. Some eat snacks. They receive last-minute advice from their coach.

Substitute Edinson Cavani of Paris Saint-Germain warms up on the sidelines during a game.

During the game, each player on the field focuses on playing his position. Defenders work on protecting against the opponent's top scorers. Midfielders keep the ball moving and join the defense or the attack. And forwards look for chances to make a run behind the defense and get a shot on goal.

In pro soccer matches, coaches can use three substitutions. This means that players on the bench need to stay loose.

They won't know if they're going to be needed until the coach calls on them.

After the game, the coaches and star players speak to media reporters. They say how they feel about the game, win or lose. They might talk about their game plan.

Players also make sure to eat healthful postgame meals. They eat within two hours of the game. It's important for them to recharge their bodies. Many players eat foods rich in proteins and carbohydrates.

Players also make sure they rest after each game. If they're playing a home game, they'll often go home. If it's an away game, they'll go to a hotel or get on an airplane to head home.

Nahomi Kawasumi of Seattle Reign FC speaks with reporters. ▶

CHAPTER 3

STAYING HEALTHY AND TRAINING

Professional soccer players must stay in shape and stay healthy. This comes naturally to many players because they play almost year-round. Professional leagues take breaks during the year so players can compete for their national teams. But even soccer players who play a lot must still take care of themselves off the field.

Soccer players do lots of strength training. Some do jumping exercises or squats to keep their legs strong. Many lift weights or do pull-ups. Other players use yoga to help quiet their minds and stay focused.

Paul Dummett of Newcastle United in England trains with his teammates at the gym. ▶

Wendie Renard, a defender on the French national team, tries cryotherapy.

Players also use new technologies to help them recover from tough workouts. Some players try cryotherapy. During cryotherapy, a person stands in a small room and turns as cold air hits her. This gets blood rushing through the person's body to keep her muscles loose.

Professional soccer players watch their diets. They often eat foods rich in carbohydrates or protein to make sure they have enough energy to practice and play games. Players try to stay away from foods with a lot of fat. Some soccer players work with professional nutritionists to plan their meals.

Some players watch videos of soccer games to prepare themselves. Bradley thinks it's important to study the game. He watches videos of other teams' games to learn about them.

At the end of a season, players take a few weeks off to relax. But soon they start working out to prepare for the next season. If they were injured during the season, they'll start with easier workouts. They slowly train more and more until they feel ready for the next soccer season.

CHAPTER 4

CONNECTING WITH FANS

Soccer fans are known for being loyal to their teams. They're also known for being rowdy. These fans stand during games. They chant and sing songs. They wave flags or make special signs to show their love for the club, country, or certain star players.

The US national soccer teams have a diehard fan group called the American Outlaws. These fans cheer together for their favorite players. There are many groups of American Outlaws across the country. They meet up before games to hang out. They welcome anyone who loves the US teams.

The American Outlaws cheer on the US Men's National Team. ▶

After games, players make it a point to show their love for the fans. Players walk over to their fans in the stands to wave or give them a round of applause. Some will exchange high fives or have quick conversations with fans sitting in the first couple of rows.

Soccer clubs and leagues around the world also connect with their communities through charity events. Some leagues tell players to go to a certain number of events during a season. Many players also go to charity events on their own. These events could include youth soccer tournaments or soccer clinics. Many players host soccer clinics to teach kids. Some help with Charity Ball, a group that brings good soccer balls to children in poor communities around the world.

Stats Spotlight
31.1 million

That's the number of Twitter followers Real Madrid had in 2018. The team from Spain is one of the best in its league, La Liga. Real Madrid has won the most titles in the Champions League, a tournament in which the best teams throughout Europe compete.

Professional Italian soccer player Jordan Lukaku helps at a charity dinner.

The future of soccer is bright. The game continues to grow in the United States and around the world. The game is easy for kids to start playing, and it remains the sport with the most young players. With more players, there's more competition. Soccer players must continue to work hard so they can one day win championships or gold medals.

YOUR TURN

Practicing soccer skills doesn't require a lot of equipment, space, or teammates. A ball is all you need to improve your foot-eye coordination.

First, hold the ball at chest height and let it bounce off the ground. Then tap the ball up with your toes before catching it again. Next, instead of catching it, let it bounce again and tap it again. The bounce will help you adjust if the ball doesn't go right where you want it. Increase the number of times you tap the ball up between bounces. Change your feet while tapping. To be a good soccer player, you must be able to use both feet!

After you feel comfortable using your toes, try tapping the ball to the inside of your foot, outside of your foot, knee, chest, and head. Doing this is called "juggling."

To practice, young
◀ soccer players only
need a ball.

GLOSSARY

carbohydrates
a substance found in foods, particularly grain foods like pasta, that provides a person's body with energy

drills
activities sports players do in practice to improve their skills

elite
the best

hydrated
to have enough water in one's body

loyal
to show constant support

meditate
to calm your mind in silence

midfielder
a soccer position that requires players to be in the middle of the field, playing between forwards and defenders

nutritionists
people who work professionally to help people eat healthfully

outlined
explained or described

rowdy
noisy and excited

scouts
people from professional or college teams who look for and choose future players

shootout
a shooting competition used as a tiebreaker in soccer

substitutions
soccer players sitting on the bench who replace players on the field

FURTHER
INFORMATION

Fédération Internationale de Football Association (FIFA)
https://www.fifa.com

Major League Soccer
https://www.mlssoccer.com

National Women's Soccer League
http://www.nwslsoccer.com

Savage, Jeff. *Soccer Super Stats*. Minneapolis: Lerner Publications, 2018.

Savage, Jeff. *US Women's National Team*. Minneapolis: Lerner Publications, 2019.

US National Soccer Teams
https://www.ussoccer.com

World Cup 2018: The Teams, The Stars, The Stories. New York: Abbeville Kids, 2018.

INDEX

ABOUT THE AUTHOR

Andy Greder is a newspaper reporter for the *Pioneer Press* in St. Paul, Minnesota. He covers Minnesota United FC, a newer club in Major League Soccer. He also covers University of Minnesota athletics, including women's soccer, basketball, and football.